SPACE
IN 30 SECONDS

An Imprint of Sterling Publishing
387 Park Avenue South
New York, NY 10016

ISBN 978-1-4351-5333-2

First published in the UK by

Ivy Press

CREATIVE DIRECTOR   Peter Bridgewater
MANAGING EDITOR   Hazel Songhurst
PROJECT EDITOR   Cath Senker
ART DIRECTOR   Kevin Knight
DESIGNER   Jane Hawkins and Lisa McCormick
ILLUSTRATORS
Melvyn Evans (color)
Marta Munoz (black and white)

Manufactured in China

Lot #: 1

2 4 6 8 10 9 7 5 3 1

[01/14]

SPACE
IN 30 SECONDS

CLIVE GIFFORD

CONSULTANT: DR. MIKE GOLDSMITH

Sandy Creek
NEW YORK

Contents

Space: What's Out There?
... in 60 seconds

When we talk about space, we are talking about the universe. The universe is everything that we can touch, feel, sense, measure, or detect. It includes living things, planets, stars, clouds of dust, and the space in between all of these objects.

Space is so incredibly vast that it is impossible for humans to explore it directly. Yet over the past 100 years, astronomers and scientists have made huge advances in their understanding of space. To make their discoveries, they use scientific instruments to gather information about distant bodies, such as stars or black holes.

To find out about planets, moons, and other bodies nearer to Earth, machines called probes are sent into space on missions of exploration. In August 2012, for example, a car-sized robot called the Curiosity Rover reached the surface of the planet Mars after a 350-million-mile (563-million-km) journey from Earth. It is going to spend at least two years exploring Earth's planetary neighbor, sending back information and photographs to Earth via radio waves.

This book looks at many important topics about space. It is divided into chapters on how the universe began and might end, stars and their different types, the sun and planets that make up the solar system, galaxies, and how humans learn about space.

Every topic has a page you can read in 30 seconds to grasp the main facts—fast. If you're in a hurry, there is a 3-second sum-up to give you the basic idea in a nutshell. And the 3-minute missions give you the chance to discover some of the principles of space for yourself, from the comfort of your home on Earth.

The Big Bang

For centuries, humans have looked to the night sky and wondered how the universe began, what shape it is, and how big it might be. Many different theories have been suggested about the start of the universe. At the present time, most cosmologists—space scientists—agree with a theory that is called the "big bang." Far less certain is how the universe might end in the distant future.

The Big Bang
Glossary

astronomer A scientist who studies the sun, moon, stars, planets, and space in general.

atom The smallest part of an **element** that can take part in a chemical change.

big bang The sudden expansion that many scientists suggest created the **universe**.

big chill One theory about how the **universe** might end, with all the stars fading away and dying.

big crunch A theory about how the **universe** might end by collapsing into one dense point.

big rip The theory that the **universe** could end by everything in it being ripped apart.

dark energy A kind of energy that scientists believe may make up more than 70 percent of the **universe** but they do not know exactly what it is.

dense Heavy in relation to its size, so that a tiny amount is extremely heavy.

element A simple chemical substance that is made up of **atoms** of only one type. It cannot be split into a simpler substance.

expansion The act of something getting bigger.

galaxy A grouping of stars, dust, and gas clouds that may also contain planets. Our galaxy is the Milky Way, which contains our sun and its planets as well as many other stars. All the stars we can see without a telescope belong to the Milky Way.

gravity A force that pulls objects in space toward each other. Around Earth, it pulls them toward the planet, so things fall to the ground when you drop them.

light-year The distance that light travels in one year.

Local Group The collection of galaxies that our **galaxy** is part of.

mass The quantity of material that something contains.

matter All the substances and objects in the **universe** that have **mass** and take up space.

nucleus The central part of an **atom** that contains most of its **mass**.

solar system The sun and all the planets and other objects that move around it.

telescope A scientific instrument that gathers in light or other signals from space to let people study distant objects.

universe The whole of space and everything in it, including Earth, the other planets, and stars.

The Universe Begins

... in 30 seconds

The universe is everything that exists. It's phenomenally huge. Imagine something as big as you can, multiply it by a billion, and you're still nowhere near how big it is.

Scientists who study the universe believe in a theory called the big bang to explain how the universe was formed.

The big bang wasn't an explosion. It was an unbelievably sudden expansion out of a single point. Everything expanded out of this single point including space, energy, and matter—all the physical things in the universe. Forces, such as gravity, formed. Time was created. There is no "before" the big bang. It's hard to make sense of the idea.

Within 3 seconds of the big bang, the three simplest elements had formed: hydrogen, helium, and lithium. The earliest stars formed between 50 and 150 million years later, followed by galaxies. Around 9 billion years after the big bang, the solar system and Earth were created.

How Old is the Universe?

It's 13,700 million years old. Imagine its history squeezed into a year on Earth.

- The big bang was within the first second of January 1.

- Earth formed in September and the first dinosaurs appeared on December 24.

- Humans appeared in the late evening on December 31. The ancient Romans arrived 4 seconds before midnight.

3-second sum-up

The universe probably began with the big bang.

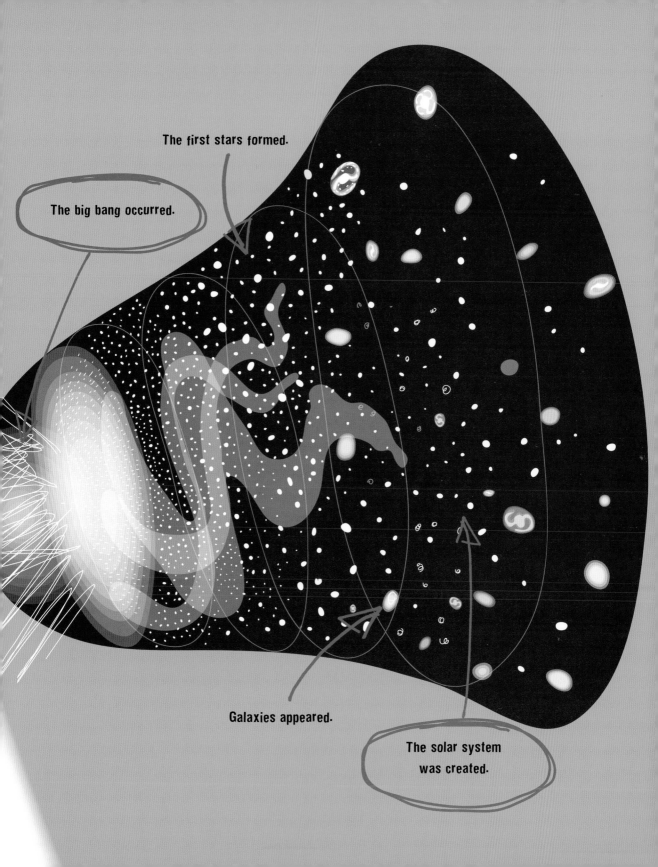

The Expanding Universe

... in 30 seconds

Ever since the big bang, the universe has been expanding and still is to this day. How did scientists find out?

In 1929, astronomer Edwin Hubble observed galaxies using the world's biggest telescope at the time. He was able to measure how groups of galaxies were moving away from other groups of galaxies.

Think of the groups of galaxies as raisins in bread dough. As the dough rises, the raisins move farther apart from each other. So, distant clusters of galaxies are moving away from our Local Group of galaxies. And the farther they are, the faster they go.

In the 1990s, scientists found that space wasn't expanding at one set speed, but that the expansion was accelerating (speeding up). Many scientists believe that this is caused by dark energy—a mysterious energy that makes up more than 70 percent of the universe.

3-second sum-up

The universe is expanding quickly.

3-minute mission Make an Expanding Universe

1 Slightly inflate a large balloon and clip a clothespin over the end to keep in the air.

2 Mark ten swirls with a marker pen on the balloon. Each swirl is a cluster of galaxies. Mark a tiny M for the Milky Way.

3 Inflate the balloon to about two-thirds its full size and see how the distances increase between the swirls.

4 Completely inflate the balloon to see the distances increase again. The swirls are not moving on the balloon. It is the balloon that is getting bigger, just like space is expanding.

Light-years

... in 30 seconds

A light-year is a unit of measurement to describe how far away objects are in space. Light moves incredibly quickly, at 186,282 miles (299,792 km) a second, and an unbelievable 5,878,625,373,200 miles (9,460,730,472,580 km)—about 6 trillion miles (9.4 trillion km)—in a year.

So one light-year is about 6 trillion miles (9.4 trillion km).

Why do we need to use light-years? Well, the universe is HUGE and distances between objects are so big that using miles or kilometers just isn't useful.

The nearest galaxy, Andromeda, is a whopping 13,000,000,000,000,000,000 miles, or 13 quintillion miles (21,000,000,000,000,000,000 km), away. Just look at those figures!

These numbers have so many figures, it's hard to work out what they mean. So astronomers use light-years instead, and would say that Andromeda is 2,300,000 light-years (2.3 million light-years) away.

3-minute mission Work out a You Year

A YOU YEAR is how far YOU would travel running 24 hours a day, 365 days a year, at full speed.

1 Time how many seconds it takes to run 100 meters.

2 Divide 100 by your time to see how many meters you travel in 1 second.

3 Multiply this by 60, then 60, then 24, then 365.

4 Divide the answer by 1,609.344 (you can use a calculator) to get the distance in miles (or 1,000 for kilometers) you would travel in a year—a YOU YEAR.

3-second sum-up

Nothing can travel faster than the speed of light.

Crunch Time

... in 30 seconds

Will the universe end? No one actually knows. If the universe continues to expand, a "big chill" could happen. Galaxies would become farther and farther apart and eventually run out of gas to make new stars.

The existing stars would run out of fuel and slowly fade away. The universe would dim and cool until it became very cold and dark.

Another more violent ending is the "big rip." In this theory, space continues to expand in the universe, but this expansion starts to occur within galaxies, causing them to separate, then in stars, pulling them apart. It would continue in planets and finally, individual atoms. Everything would be ripped apart by the expansion.

This all sounds awful, but relax. No scientist is predicting the end of the universe anytime soon. Any ending is billions of years away.

3-second sum-up

The universe might end by freezing, ripping apart, or collapsing completely.

The Big Crunch

In the past, one popular theory for the end of the universe was the "big crunch."

The idea was that the universe could expand by only a certain amount before the force of gravity started to pull it back, just like a rubber band.

Everything in the universe would become closer and closer until the universe collapsed into one extremely dense point.

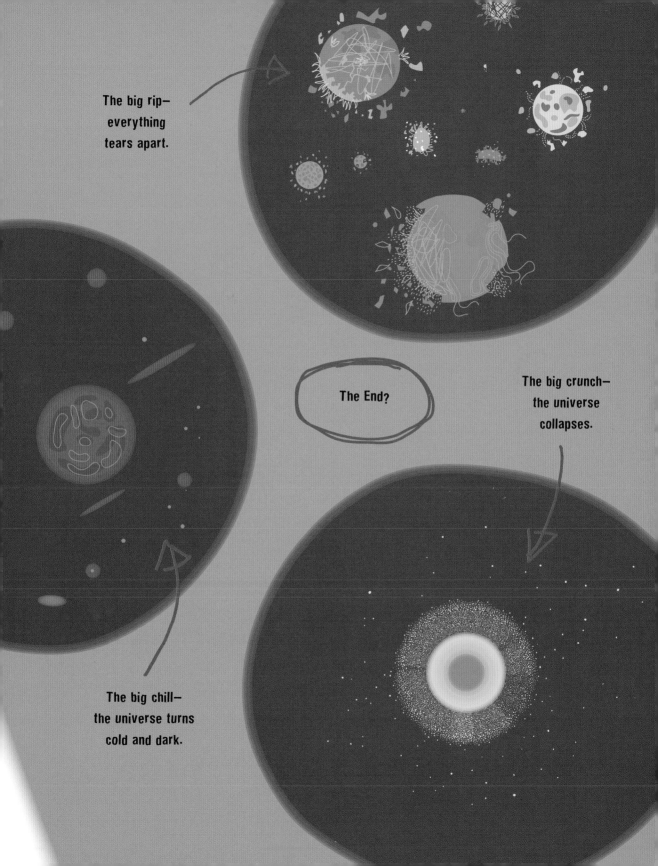

The big rip—
everything
tears apart.

The big crunch—
the universe
collapses.

The End?

The big chill—
the universe turns
cold and dark.

Stars

Stars are giant balls of gas that burn fiercely. The smallest may be one-tenth of the size of our sun. The largest may be more than 100 times bigger! We can see thousands of stars in the night sky from Earth. However, they are just a tiny fraction of the total number in the universe—scientists believe there are billions and billions of them.

Stars
Glossary

apparent magnitude How bright a star looks from Earth.

astronomer A scientist who studies the sun, moon, stars, planets, and space in general.

atom The smallest part of an element (a simple chemical substance) that can take part in a chemical change.

constellation A group of stars that forms a shape in the sky and has a name.

dense Heavy in relation to its size, so that a tiny amount is extremely heavy.

diameter A straight line from one side of a circle across the middle to the other side.

galaxy A grouping of stars, dust, and gas clouds that may also have planets. Our galaxy is the Milky Way, which contains our sun and its planets as well as many other stars. All the stars we can see without a telescope belong to the Milky Way.

gravity A force that pulls objects in space toward each other. Around Earth, it pulls them toward the planet, so things fall to the ground when you drop them.

light-year The distance that light travels in one year.

mass The quantity of material that something contains.

matter All the substances and objects in the **universe** that have **mass** and take up space.

nebula (plural nebulae) A huge cloud of dust and gas. Some nebulae form stars.

neutron A very small piece of **matter** that forms part of the **nucleus** of an **atom**.

neutron star A type of extremely dense star.

nuclear fusion When the **nuclei** of **atoms** are fused together (combined) to form a larger **nucleus** and energy is released.

nuclear reaction When the nuclei of **atoms** are changed from one element into another.

nucleus (plural nuclei) The part in the center of an **atom** that contains most of its **mass**.

orbit A curved path followed by a planet (or an object) as it moves around a planet or a star. To orbit is to go around another planet or star.

Orion nebula One of the closest **nebulae** to Earth.

planetary nebula When some stars die, a cloud called a planetary **nebula** is formed. The core then forms a **white dwarf** and eventually the star fades away.

pressure The force or weight with which something presses against something else.

protostar A clump of matter (substance) that forms as part of the birth of a star.

red dwarf A small star that is not very hot.

red giant A large star toward the end of its life that is really cool for a star and gives out a reddish light.

solar system The sun and all the planets and other objects that move around it.

supernova, type II (plural supernovae) A star that suddenly becomes much brighter and gives out a huge amount of energy because it is exploding and will die.

universe The whole of space and everything in it, including Earth, the other planets, and stars.

white dwarf A small star that has died and is very **dense**.

Star Birth
... in 30 seconds

Some nebulae form stars. Nebulae are gigantic clouds of dust and gas found throughout the universe.

The Orion nebula is one of the closest to Earth, about 1,340 light-years away. It's more than 24 light-years wide, that's—wait for it—more than 141,000,000,000,000 miles (227,000,000,000,000 km)!

A local supernova (star explosion) or another star passing close by can trigger parts of the cloud to start to contract under the force of its own gravity. As the parts become smaller and draw in more dust and gas, they become denser and hotter and form a clump of matter called a protostar.

The core starts to collapse in on itself, increasing in pressure and temperature, and causing nuclear fusion. This fuses hydrogen atoms together into helium atoms and produces huge amounts of energy. Out of the protostar, a star forms.

3-second sum-up

Stars are born in giant star nurseries called nebulae.

3-minute mission Go Star Hunting

Constellations are patterns of stars we can see in the night sky. The constellations change their positions throughout the year.

Copy out a star map from a book or print one out from an astronomy website. (There are several astronomy websites especially for kids on the internet.)

On a clear night, try to find three constellations.

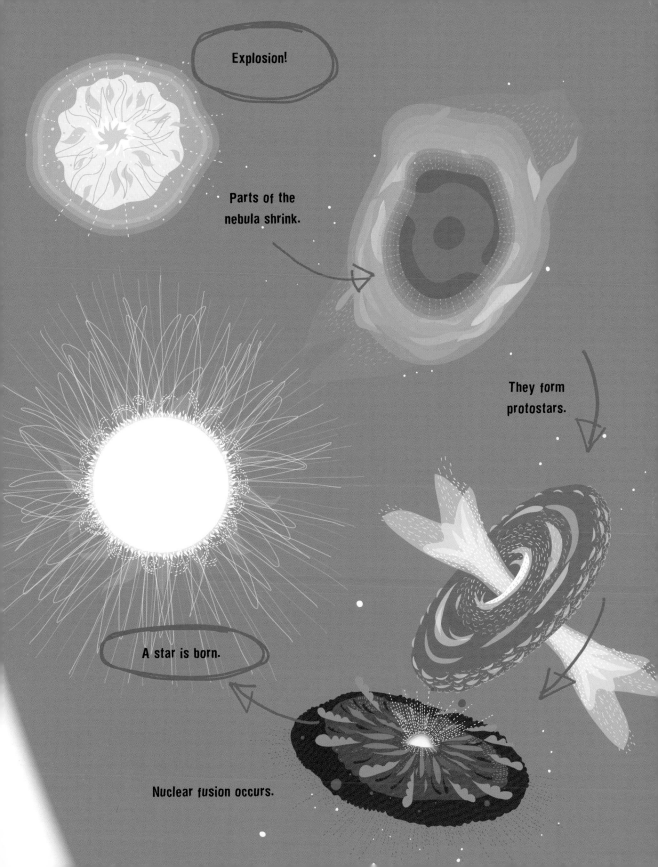

Types of Stars

... in 30 seconds

Stars vary in size, temperature, and how bright they appear from Earth.

The sun is a pretty average star in size. Some are smaller; others are far larger. Betelgeuse (betel-jooz), in the Orion constellation, is a gigantic star. If Betelgeuse replaced our sun, its outer surface would extend out as far as the orbit of Jupiter!

Other stars are even larger. VY Canis Majoris, in the constellation Canis Major, is the largest known star. Scientists believe it is 1,900 million miles (3,000 million km) in diameter—more than 2,000 times the diameter of the sun.

Stars burn at different temperatures. Astronomers group stars into classes called spectral types, depending on how hot they are. Type O is the hottest, with surface temperatures of above 30,000°Kelvin, or about 53,500°F (30,000°C). That's hot!

Only around 1 in 3 million stars are Type O, and they tend to shine extremely brightly. Lying some 5,000 light-years from us, the Type O star Cygnus OB2-12 is 6 million times brighter than our sun.

3-second sum-up

Some stars are bigger, brighter, and hotter than others.

How Brightly Do They Shine?

Stars can also be classified by how brightly they appear to shine to us as we view them from Earth. This classification is called "apparent magnitude."

The sun is, of course, the brightest star, followed by Sirius, the brightest in the night sky, then Canopus and Arcturus.

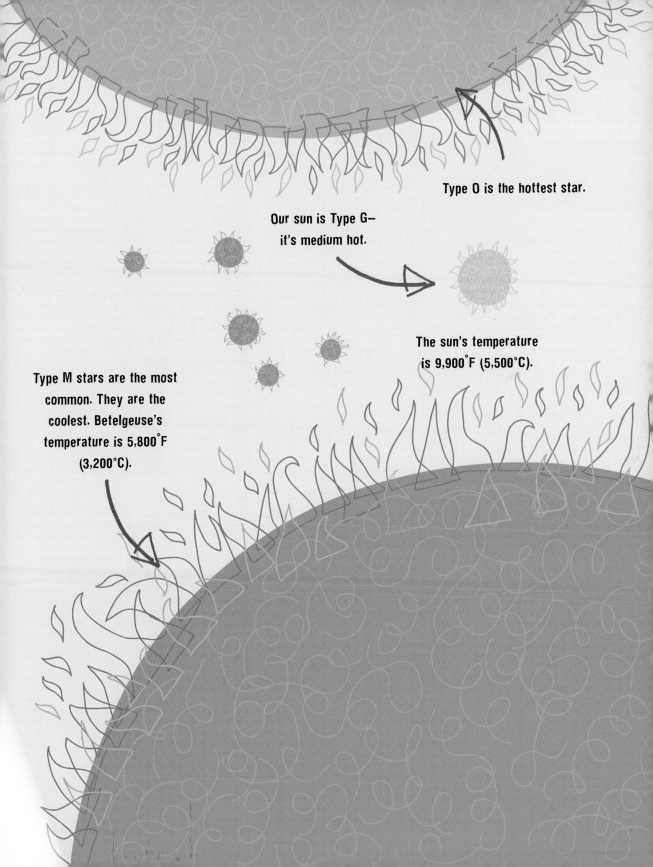

Type O is the hottest star.

Our sun is Type G—
it's medium hot.

The sun's temperature
is 9,900°F (5,500°C).

Type M stars are the most
common. They are the
coolest. Betelgeuse's
temperature is 5,800°F
(3,200°C).

Supernovae

... in 30 seconds

Stars die in different ways. One of the most spectacular ways is a type II supernova. This occurs when a massive star no longer has enough fuel to keep nuclear fusion occurring at its core (center). The core collapses sharply under the force of gravity and incredible temperatures are generated—as high as 180 billion°F (100 billion°C).

The core of the supernova rebounds, sending matter hurtling out into space as fast as 9,000 to 25,000 miles (15,000 to 40,000 km) per second. In one second, a supernova can generate as much energy as a small star does in its lifetime. Some supernovae continue to shine 10 billion times as brightly as a normal star for months.

Supernovae are rare events to find, but keep your eyes peeled when stargazing and you never know. In 2011, Kathryn Aurora Gray, a 10-year-old Canadian schoolgirl, became the youngest person ever to discover a new supernova, occurring 240 million light-years away in a galaxy called UGC3378.

3-second sum-up

A type II supernova is a giant explosion that rips a star apart.

3-minute mission The Supernova Effect

See how energy from the rebounding core of a supernova forces away the outer layers of a star:

1 Drop a basketball (or soccer ball) and a tennis ball on hard ground one at a time, noting how far they bounce.

2 Next, hold the tennis ball (outer layers of a star) on top of the basketball (star's core). Drop them together.

3 The tennis ball will fly away with great force, just as the outer layers of a star are blown away by the core in a supernova.

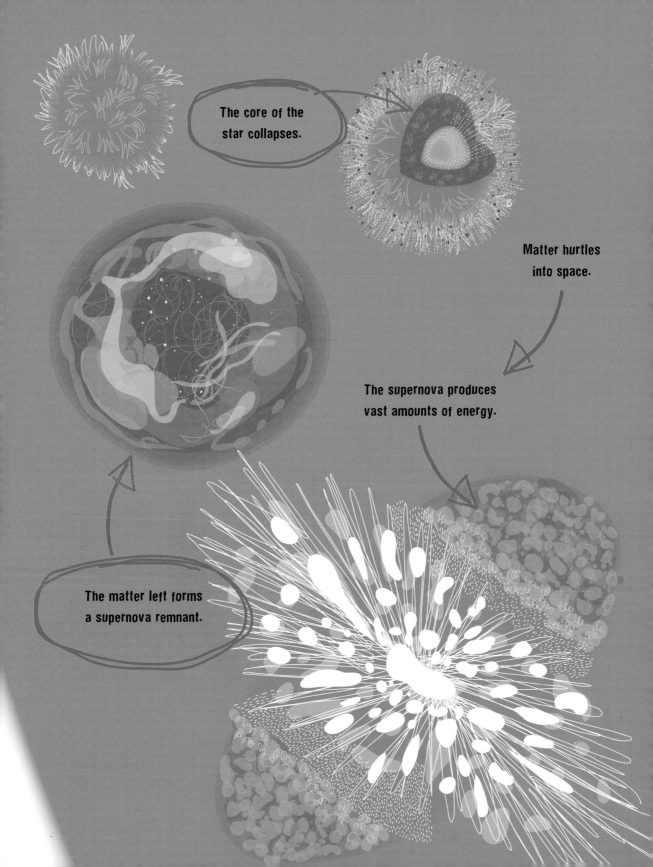

The core of the star collapses.

Matter hurtles into space.

The supernova produces vast amounts of energy.

The matter left forms a supernova remnant.

Quiet Star Death

... in 30 seconds

Stars don't all end in spectacular supernovae. Red dwarfs are stars with less than half of the sun's mass but still have nuclear reactions in their core. These stars have quiet endings, gradually shrinking and growing dim as they run out of fuel.

Stars between half and eight times the mass of the sun have more complex endings.

As they exhaust their hydrogen fuel at their center, they start using helium as fuel and swell in size, becoming red giants. Eventually, they cast off their outer shell or layers to form a cloud called a planetary nebula. The core is called a white dwarf.

White dwarfs are small, extremely dense stars mostly made of carbon. A typical white dwarf is around the same size or slightly bigger than Earth but contains as much matter as the sun. A white dwarf will slowly cool and fade over many billions of years.

3-second sum-up

Some stars shrink and die out while others swell then cool.

Neutron Stars

White dwarfs are dense, but neutron stars are even denser. Neutron stars are formed from a supernova that leaves an unbelievably dense core of neutrons.

A teaspoon of neutron star might weigh more than 1 million tons. A neutron star may be less than 12 miles (20 km) in diameter but contain as much matter as the entire solar system.

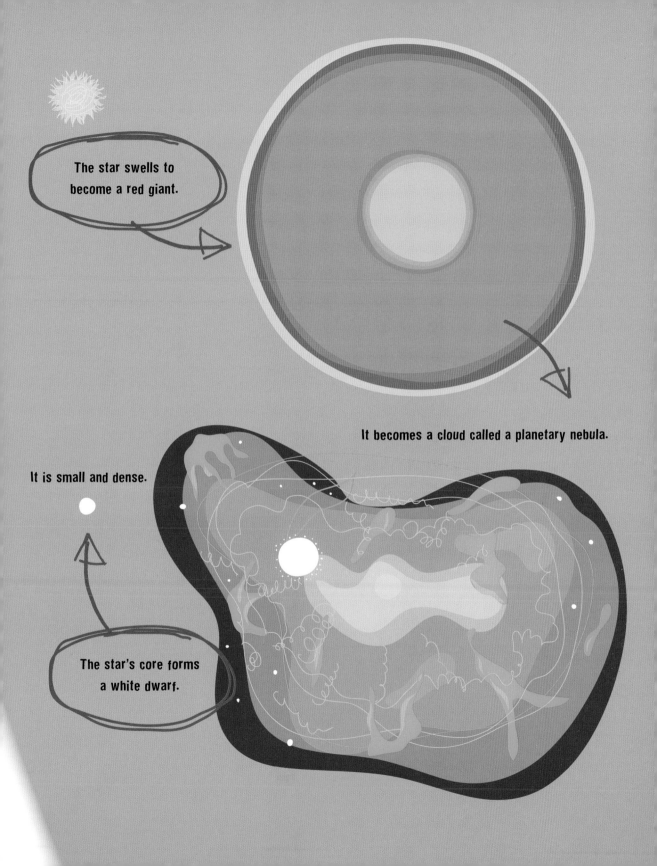

The star swells to become a red giant.

It becomes a cloud called a planetary nebula.

It is small and dense.

The star's core forms a white dwarf.

Sun and Inner Planets

The sun is an average-sized star moving through space. The pull of its gravity keeps eight planets, their moons, and other bodies traveling around it along elliptical (oval) paths called orbits. The four planets closest to the sun are Mercury, Venus, Earth, and Mars. They are called the terrestrial planets because they have solid, rocky surfaces. These, along with the sun, asteroids, comets, dust, gas, and meteoroids make up the inner solar system.

Sun and Inner Planets
Glossary

asteroid A small body of rock, metal, or both that **orbits** the sun.

astronomer A scientist who studies the sun, moon, stars, planets, and space in general.

astronomical unit (AU) A unit of distance. 1 AU equals 93 million miles (149.6 million km), approximately the distance between the middle of Earth and the middle of the sun.

atmosphere The mixture of gases that surrounds a planet.

atom The smallest part of an element (a simple chemical substance) that can take part in a chemical change.

axis An imaginary line through the middle of an object, such as a planet, around which the object turns.

canyon A deep valley with steep sides of rock.

chromosphere The sun's inner **atmosphere**. Chromosphere means "sphere of color."

convective zone An inner layer of the sun, after the **radiative** layer.

corona The outer **atmosphere** of the sun, which is bigger than the sun itself.

crater A large hole in the ground, it can be caused by something big hitting it from space, such as an **asteroid**.

diameter A straight line from one side of a circle across the center to the other side.

dwarf planet A large object in space, such as Pluto, that goes around the sun but is not as large as a planet.

gravity A force that pulls objects in space toward each other. Around Earth, it pulls them toward the planet, so things fall to the ground when you drop them.

maria The rocky plains on the moon.

mass The quantity of material that something contains.

mph or km/h Miles or kilometers per hour; a measure of speed.

nuclear reaction When the nuclei of **atoms** are changed from one element (simple chemical substance) into another.

orbit A curved path followed by a planet (or an object) as it moves around a planet or a star. To orbit is to go around another planet or star.

photosphere The surface of the sun that you can see.

polar ice cap A layer of ice permanently covering parts of Earth, and Mars, around the North and South poles.

pressure The force or weight with which something presses against something else.

radiative layer The part of the sun next to the core. Heat from the core is transferred through the radiative layer outward.

rotation The action of an object moving in a circle around a centered point, for example, Earth spinning on its **axis**.

solar system The sun and all the planets and other objects that move around it.

space probe A spacecraft without people on board that obtains information and sends it back to Earth.

telescope A scientific instrument that gathers in light or other signals from space, helping people to study distant objects.

volcanic lava Hot, liquid rock that comes out of a volcano.

35

The Sun

... in 30 seconds

The sun is the star at the heart of the solar system. Its great mass creates the gravity that keeps planets, asteroids, and other bodies orbiting around it. It provides heat and light.

In its core, the sun is a giant nuclear furnace. Every second, there are nuclear reactions. More than 600 million tons of hydrogen atoms are fused together to create helium atoms and vast amounts of energy.

This energy travels through the sun's radiative and convective layers to its surface—the photosphere. Above the photosphere lies the chromosphere, then the outer atmosphere—the corona. The corona can reach temperatures of 1.8–3.6 million°F (1–2 million°C). HOT!

3-minute mission Measure the Sun

Measure the sun with a thin piece of cardboard, a pin, white paper, and ruler. **Remember: Never look directly at the sun!**

1 Make a pinhole in the middle of the cardboard and hold it so that sunlight shines through the hole onto the white paper. Try to get as much distance as possible between the cardboard and paper to create a bigger image (3 feet/1 meter or more is ideal).

2 Get a friend to measure the diameter of the image on the paper and the distance from the pinhole to the paper. Add these figures to the math equation below.

$$\frac{\text{Diameter of sun on paper}}{\text{Distance from pinhole to paper}} \times 92{,}960{,}000 \text{ miles}/149{,}600{,}000 \text{ km} \text{ (Earth to sun distance)} = \text{Diameter of sun in miles/km}$$

How close were you to the sun's real size?

3-second sum-up

The sun gives heat and light to our solar system.

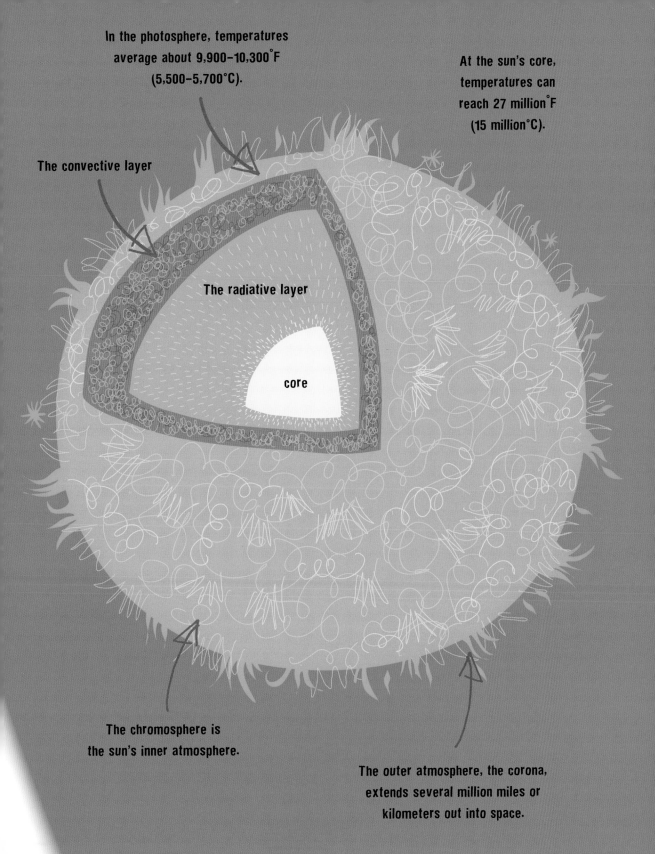

In the photosphere, temperatures average about 9,900–10,300°F (5,500–5,700°C).

At the sun's core, temperatures can reach 27 million°F (15 million°C).

The convective layer

The radiative layer

core

The chromosphere is the sun's inner atmosphere.

The outer atmosphere, the corona, extends several million miles or kilometers out into space.

Mercury
... in 30 seconds

Mercury is the closest planet to the sun. On average, it is 36 million miles (57.9 million km) from the sun. Mercury is the smallest planet in our solar system.

Mercury's orbit around the sun takes just 88 Earth days to complete, so its year is one-quarter of the length of Earth's.

All planets spin on their axis and a complete rotation is known as a day. A day on Earth lasts almost 24 hours, but on Mercury, which spins very slowly, a full rotation takes more than 1,400 hours to complete—that's more than 58 days on Earth. So there are less than two Mercury days to its year.

Temperatures on Mercury can reach up to 800°F (427°C) when the sun strikes directly. Out of the sun's rays, they can drop below -274°F (-170°C).

Large parts of the planet's surface are covered in craters of various sizes. Astronomers believe that Mercury was bombarded by asteroids during the early stages of the solar system's formation.

3-second sum-up

Tiny Mercury can be baking hot or freezing cold.

3-minute mission Make Craters

Mix flour and a little water in a mixing bowl to form a soft but not runny mixture. Fill a large baking pan or casserole dish with the mixture and take it outside.

Standing directly above the bowl, drop different-sized round objects (such as a marble and a golf ball) into the pan from knee, chest, and above-head height. Note the different sizes of craters formed by different objects impacting on the surface at different speeds.

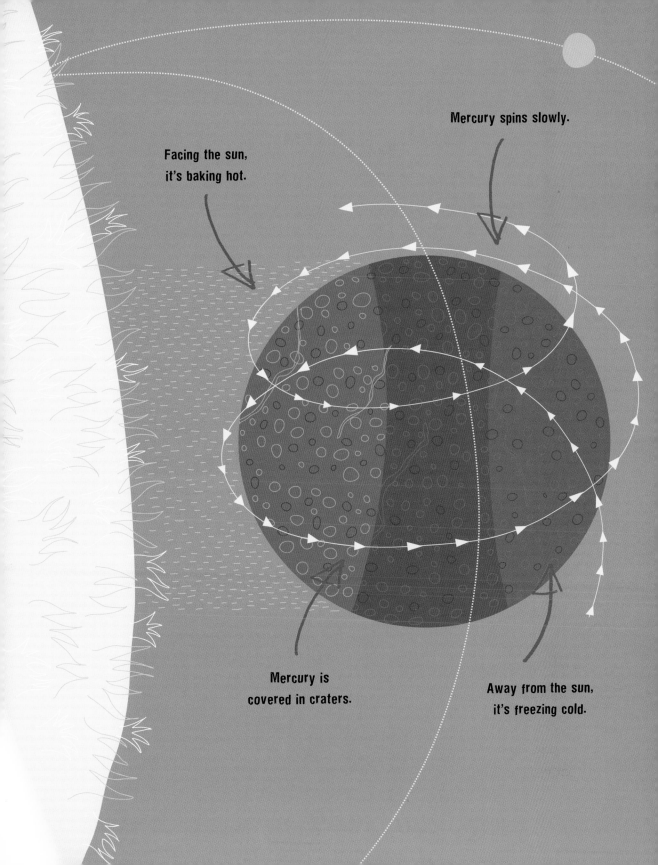

Facing the sun,
it's baking hot.

Mercury spins slowly.

Mercury is
covered in craters.

Away from the sun,
it's freezing cold.

Venus

... in 30 seconds

Venus is the second closest planet to the sun and is a similar size to Earth. It's the hottest planet in the solar system.

Venus takes 224.7 Earth days to complete an orbit around the sun, which is really quick. However, when it comes to turning on its own axis, Venus is a serious slow coach. It takes a staggering 243 Earth days to complete a rotation. Its day is longer than its year.

Venus has an average surface temperature of about 864°F (462°C)—that's more than enough to melt the metal lead.

There's little letup either, because its atmosphere acts like a really thick blanket, keeping in all that heat. Venus' atmosphere is about 96 percent carbon dioxide, 3.5 percent nitrogen, some sulfur, and almost no oxygen or water vapor—substances needed for animal life.

The thick atmosphere presses down on the surface with 90 times more pressure than Earth's atmosphere. Even if you survived a descent through the poisonous clouds of gases, the pressure on the surface of Venus would squash you flat.

3-second sum-up

Venus is extremely hot with a poisonous atmosphere.

Visiting Venus

The thick, toxic atmosphere makes it difficult for astronomers to view the surface of Venus from Earth, but space probes, such as Magellan, Venus Express, and the Venera series of probes, have reached and studied Venus, using instruments that scan through the clouds.

They found a lifeless surface littered with volcanoes, some craters, and plains made of volcanic lava.

Its thick, toxic atmosphere
keeps Venus in sweltering heat.

The atmosphere is
90 times heavier
than Earth's.

Space probes can
examine Venus close up.

Venus has volcanoes,
craters, and lava plains.

Earth and Moon

... in 30 seconds

Earth lies an average of 92,955,807 miles (149,597,870.7 km) from the sun. That figure equals 1 astronomical unit (AU), a unit of measurement used in the solar system. For example, Jupiter is around 5.2 AU from the sun.

Our planet is seriously on the move, whizzing through space on its 584-million-mile (939.9-million-km) orbit round the sun. As it orbits, Earth also turns on its own axis. It turns to face the sun every 23 hours, 56 minutes, and 4 seconds, giving us our day and night.

Earth is tilted at an angle of 23.5 degrees. This tilt creates the seasons. The hemisphere (half) of Earth tilted more toward the sun enjoys summer while the other half experiences winter. As Earth continues its orbit, the seasons change.

Surrounding the planet, and protecting it from many of the sun's harmful rays, is Earth's atmosphere. The atmosphere keeps Earth's surface warm and enables life to function.

Earth's one moon is an average of 0.0026 AU (238,855 miles/ 384,400 km) away from Earth. It is marked with hundreds of craters and flattish, rocky plains called maria.

3-second sum-up

You're standing on a body traveling at about 66,500 mph (107,000 km/h) around the sun.

3-minute mission Make a Moon Map

Get a set of binoculars or a telescope, pick a night with good, clear skies, and make your own moon map, sketching out any features you can see. Can you find any craters or maria?

Earth is tilted as it orbits the sun.

The moon has craters and rocky plains called maria.

The half of Earth tilted toward the sun has summer.

The half of Earth tilted away from the sun has winter.

Earth's axis

Mars

... in 30 seconds

Mars is the second smallest planet in the solar system—it's just over half the size of Earth. With no seas of liquid water on its surface, it has about as much land as our planet. Much of this looks like a rocky, dusty desert strewn with craters and plains.

Yet, in places, Mars boasts some of the solar system's most spectacular features: a gigantic canyon system called the Valles Marineris, a huge volcano, and a massive crater.

In comparison to these giant features, Mars' two moons are puny. Deimos and Phobos are not round and are shaped similar to two large potatoes. Phobos, the larger moon, has an average diameter of 16 miles (27 km).

Scientists have discovered the features of Mars using telescopes and visiting space probes. They have found that Mars' atmosphere is thin and more than 95 percent of it is carbon dioxide. The planet has polar ice caps, made mostly of frozen carbon dioxide. Scientists have found frozen water on Mars, too.

3-second sum-up

Our close neighbor, Mars, contains desert, ice, volcanoes, and craters.

3-minute mission Journey to Mars

A manned mission to and from Mars with some meaningful time on the planet might take three or more years. What would such a mission be like for explorers?

Try to list some of the challenges you think would be involved in traveling for so long, and list five personal items you would take with you on such a long journey. Remember that most of the room in the spacecraft will be packed with supplies for the journey.

Olympus Mons is the solar system's biggest volcano.

Phobos

The Valles Marineris is so large it would span the entire USA.

Deimos

Mars' southerly polar ice cap

The Hellas Planitia is an enormous crater.

Asteroids and Dwarf Planets

... in 30 seconds

Asteroids are chunks of rock, metal, or a mixture of both that orbit the sun. Many are found in the main belt—a giant, donut-shaped ring between Mars and Jupiter thought to contain more than a million asteroids greater than 1,000 yards (1 km) in diameter.

These are believed to be leftovers from the solar system's formation—chunks of material that never made it into a planet.

Asteroids are also found elsewhere in the solar system. The Trojans are asteroids found along the path Jupiter takes as it orbits the sun. There are also near-Earth asteroids, which are found inside Mars' orbit round the sun.

When Clyde Tombaugh, an American astronomer, discovered Pluto in 1930, it was classified as the ninth planet in the solar system. In 2006, scientists reclassified Pluto as a dwarf planet. These are bodies that are basically round in shape, orbit the sun, but are not big enough to sweep all other material out of their path.

3-second sum-up

Asteroids are chunks of rock and metal. Dwarf planets are too small to be planets.

3-minute mission Space Probe Check

Two space probes, Dawn and New Horizons, are set to visit two dwarf planets in 2015. Visit the NASA space probe Web page at http://solarsystem.nasa.gov/missions

Click on the target button and select dwarf planets from the drop-down menu. Check which ones are being visited and which other asteroid Dawn has already traveled to.

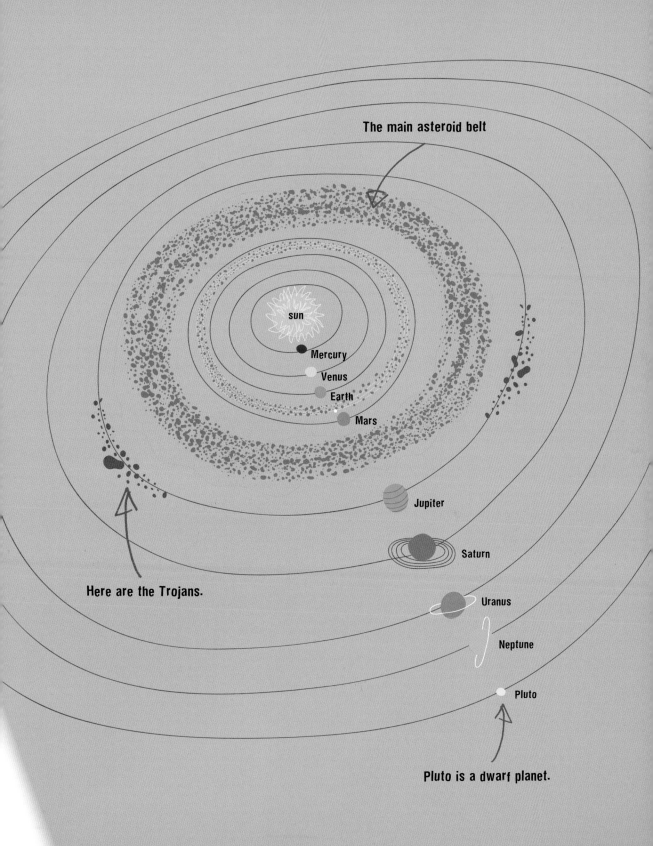

The main asteroid belt

sun

Mercury

Venus

Earth

Mars

Jupiter

Saturn

Uranus

Neptune

Pluto

Here are the Trojans.

Pluto is a dwarf planet.

Outer Solar System

Past Mars and the asteroid belt lies the outer solar system. This vast region of space is home to the four gas giant planets—Jupiter, Saturn, Uranus, and Neptune—and their many moons. Large numbers of comets are found here, too. Beyond Neptune lies a number of small bodies, including the Kuiper Belt objects and dwarf planets, such as Pluto, Haumea, and Eris. Far from the sun, this region of the solar system is freezing cold.

Outer Solar System
Glossary

astronomical unit (AU)
A unit of distance. 1 AU equals 93 million miles (149.6 million km), approximately the distance between the middle of Earth and the middle of the sun.

atmosphere The mixture of gases that surround a planet.

axis An imaginary line through the middle of an object, such as a planet, around which the object turns.

coma The cloud of dust and gases around the core of a **comet**.

comet A mass of ice and dust that moves around the sun.

dense Heavy in relation to its size, so that a tiny amount is extremely heavy.

diameter A straight line from one side of a circle across the center to the other side.

element A simple chemical substance that is made up of atoms (the smallest parts of an element) of only one type. It cannot be split into a simpler substance.

equator An imaginary line around the middle of a planet at an equal distance from the North and South poles. The poles are the two points at the opposite ends of the line on which a planet turns.

gravity A force that pulls objects in space toward each other. Around Earth, it pulls them toward the planet, so things fall to the ground when you drop them.

km/h Kilometers per hour; a measure of speed.

Kuiper Belt An area of the solar system beyond Neptune, where **comets** are found.

mass The quantity of material that something contains.

mph Miles per hour; a measure of speed.

nucleus The part in the center of an atom (the smallest part of an element) that contains most of its mass.

Oort Cloud An area that scientists believe exists way beyond the **Kuiper Belt**, and where **comets** could be found.

orbit A curved path followed by a planet (or any object) as it moves around a planet or a star. To orbit is to go around another planet or star.

pole One of the two points at the opposite ends of the line on which a planet turns.

solar system The sun and all the planets and other objects that move around it.

space probe A spacecraft without people on board that obtains information and sends it back to Earth.

telescope A scientific instrument that gathers in light or other signals from space to allow people to study distant objects.

Jupiter

... in 30 seconds

Make no mistake about it, Jupiter is massive. The largest planet in the solar system, Jupiter has a diameter of about 88,900 miles (143,000 km) across its equator. It is so large that all the other planets put together would total just 40 percent of Jupiter's mass.

For its enormous size, Jupiter rotates about its own axis at seriously high speed, about 27,000 mph (43,000 km/h).

Jupiter is a gas giant, mostly made up of hydrogen and helium, which many scientists think surrounds a small rocky core. As you get close to the center, the gases turn to liquid.

Storms rage through the planet's atmosphere, and none come bigger than the Great Red Spot, a storm with 310 mph (500 km/h) winds, which has been observed for more than 300 years. It varies in size but is currently about 12,000 miles (20,000 km) by 7,000 miles (12,000 km)—far bigger than Earth.

Jupiter's powerful gravity keeps more than 60 moons in orbit around the planet.

3-second sum-up

Gigantic Jupiter is mostly made of gas.

3-minute mission Interplanetary Weigh-in

Weight measures how strongly gravity pulls on objects. To find your weight on another planet, first weigh yourself on a scale, then multiply your weight by the planet's gravity relative to Earth's gravity, listed below.

Mercury	0.38	Venus	0.91
Mars	0.38	Jupiter	2.54
Saturn	1.08	Uranus	0.91
Neptune	1.19	Pluto	0.06

Jupiter is mainly made of gas.

Jupiter has rings—
but not as impressive
as Saturn's.

Callisto

Europa

Io

Jupiter's largest
moons are Io,
Europa, Ganymede,
and Callisto.

The Great Red Spot is
a huge, violent storm.

Ganymede

Jupiter's diameter is
about 11 times the
size of Earth's.

Earth

Saturn

... in 30 seconds

Saturn is the second largest planet in the solar system. You could fit more than 760 Earth-sized objects inside Saturn. The planet is mostly made up of hydrogen and helium gas—two of the lightest elements in the universe.

Saturn is the least dense of all the planets, only about 70 percent as dense as water. That means it would float in your bath, if your bathtub was big enough.

Jupiter, Uranus, and Neptune all have rings, but Saturn's are the biggest and most spectacular. Using space probes and scientific instruments, scientists have found they are made of billions of small rock, ice, and dust particles held in place by Saturn's gravity.

3-second sum-up

Saturn is enormous but is so light it could float in water.

3-minute mission Walk the Solar System

You'll need a large field and nine balls. First, place a ball for the sun. Measure a half-yard pace and work out how many paces to walk for each planet, using the guide below. Walk the solar system as far as Saturn (and to Uranus and Neptune if you have room).

The scale you are using is about 1 yard to every 21.9 million yards (1 meter to every 20 million kilometers). The real solar system is a staggering 20 billion times larger than your model.

Mercury	3 yd	Venus	5½ yd	Earth	7.5 yd
Mars	11½ yd	Jupiter	39 yd	Saturn	71½ yd
Uranus	143½ yd	Neptune	225 yd		

Saturn takes 29.5 years
to complete an orbit.

The sun

More than 60 moons
are orbiting Saturn.

Titan is the largest
moon—it may have
water.

Saturn has
enormous rings.

Uranus and Neptune

... in 30 seconds

Neptune is so far from the sun that it takes sunlight more than 4 hours to reach Neptune. (It takes 8 minutes to reach Earth.) Uranus and Neptune receive a tiny fraction of the sun's energy. As a result, they are extremely cold, with cloud surface temperatures dropping below -346°F (-210°C). That's seriously cold.

Fierce storms rage across Neptune, driven by the most powerful winds found in the solar system. Some have been measured traveling at 930 mph (1,500 km/h)—faster than a jet airliner on Earth.

Uranus takes 84.2 years to complete its journey around the sun. Neptune takes another 80 years to make a full orbit. So, you would have to be over 164 Earth years old to celebrate your first birthday on Neptune.

Uranus is tilted on its side, at an angle of 97.86 degrees. At its poles, summer and winter last 42 years, until the planet has completed half of its orbit and the other half of Uranus faces the sun.

3-second sum-up

Uranus and Neptune are bitterly cold planets with many moons.

Multiple Moons

Uranus and Neptune have many moons. More have been discovered in recent years as telescopes have improved and space probes have visited the region.

At the latest count, Uranus has 27. Neptune has 13, including Triton, the coldest moon in the solar system. Its surface is made of frozen nitrogen, carbon dioxide, and water ice (ice made from water).

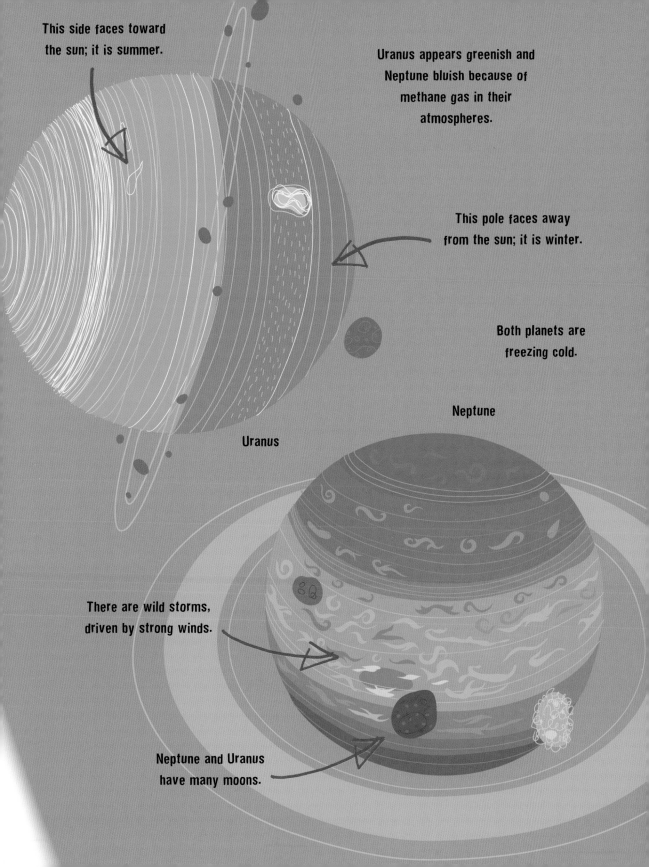

This side faces toward
the sun; it is summer.

Uranus appears greenish and
Neptune bluish because of
methane gas in their
atmospheres.

This pole faces away
from the sun; it is winter.

Both planets are
freezing cold.

Neptune

Uranus

There are wild storms,
driven by strong winds.

Neptune and Uranus
have many moons.

Comets

... in 30 seconds

You can imagine comets as dirty snowballs flying through space! They consist of ice and rock particles that form a solid nucleus, or core. Comets vary in size. The nucleus can be from a few hundred yards (or meters) up to 25 miles (40 km) in diameter. These bodies orbit the sun. For much of their journey, that's all there is to them.

Most comets are in the remotest parts of the solar system. The Kuiper Belt is an area of the solar system extending beyond Neptune for another 25 AU (25 times the distance between Earth and the sun). Way, way beyond Neptune and the Kuiper Belt may lie the Oort Cloud, some 50,000 AU away from the sun.

A passing star may dislodge a comet, sending it toward the sun. When a comet reaches around 6 AU from the sun, warmth from the sun heats up the nucleus. Some of the ice turns into gases, forming a large cloud around the nucleus called a coma, which can be 1,000 times bigger than the nucleus.

3-second sum-up

Comets are snowballs of ice and dust, hurtling around the sun.

Comet's Tails

Parts of the nucleus evaporate into gases while dust is dragged from the nucleus. Together, they can form a long tail that always faces away from the sun—or two tails.

Discovered in 1996, Comet Hyakutake's tail was found to be greater than 342 million miles (550 million km) long—more than three times the distance between the sun and Earth.

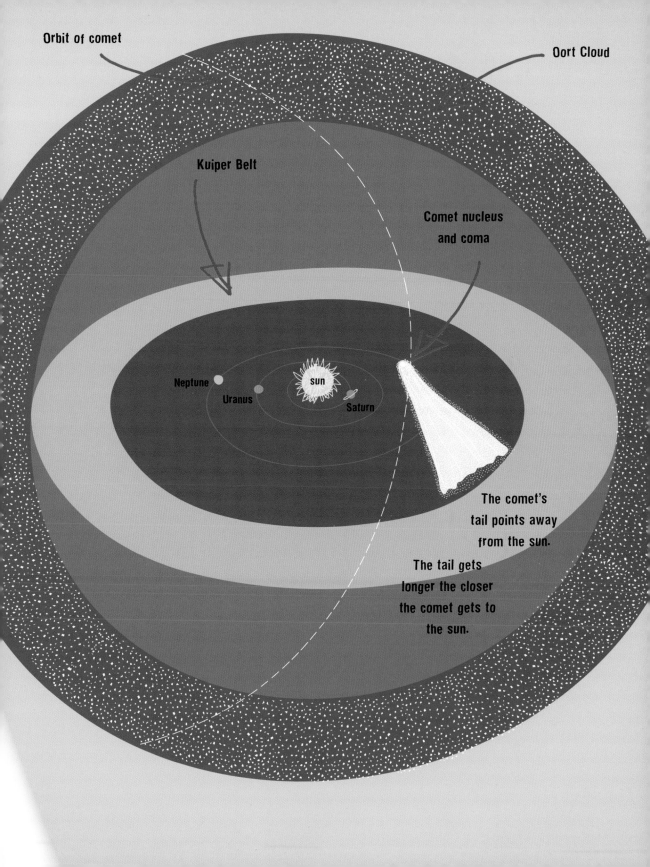

Orbit of comet

Oort Cloud

Kuiper Belt

Comet nucleus
and coma

Neptune

Uranus

sun

Saturn

The comet's
tail points away
from the sun.

The tail gets
longer the closer
the comet gets to
the sun.

What Else is Out There?

Beyond the solar system lie vast numbers of other stars in large groups called galaxies. Some galaxies are thought to contain billions of stars as well as planets and other mysterious bodies—such as black holes, from which no light can escape. There is plenty of debate over whether Earth is the only place in the universe where life flourishes. Does alien life exist somewhere out there?

What Else is Out There?
Glossary

astronomer A scientist who studies the sun, moon, stars, planets, and space in general.

black hole An area in space that nothing, not even light, can escape from, because **gravity** is so strong there.

dense Heavy in relation to its size, so that a tiny amount is extremely heavy.

element A simple chemical substance that is made up of atoms (the smallest part of an element) of only one type. It cannot be split into a simpler substance.

extraterrestrial Not from Earth.

event horizon The edge of the area around a **black hole**. Everything within the event horizon is sucked into the black hole.

exoplanet A planet in another planetary system.

galaxy A grouping of stars, dust, and gas clouds that may also contain planets. Our galaxy is the **Milky Way**, which contains our sun and its planets as well as many other stars. All the stars we can see without a telescope belong to the Milky Way.

gravity A force that pulls objects in space toward each other. Around Earth, it pulls them toward the planet, so things fall to the ground when you drop them.

light-year The distance that light travels in one year.

Local Group The collection of galaxies that our **galaxy** is part of.

Milky Way Our home **galaxy**, a system of stars that contains planets and a sun.

orbit A curved path followed by a planet (or an object) as it moves around a planet or a star. To orbit is to go around another planet or star.

solar system The sun and all the planets and other objects that move around it.

supernova, type II (plural supernovae) A star that suddenly becomes much brighter and gives out a huge amount of energy because it is exploding and will die.

telescope A scientific instrument that gathers in light or other signals from space, helping people to study distant objects.

universe The whole of space and everything in it, including Earth, the other planets, and stars.

The Milky Way
... in 30 seconds

Earth's home galaxy is the Milky Way. It is a spiral galaxy that is between 100,000 and 120,000 light-years wide and approximately 1,000 light-years thick.

To give an idea of this size, if the Milky Way was shrunk to about the size of a 100-yard (100-meter) football field, the whole solar system would be a $\frac{1}{10}$-inch (2-mm) grain of sand on it.

Just like the planets travel around the sun, our solar system travels around the center of the Milky Way. It takes between 225 and 230 million years to complete an orbit.

The Milky Way is part of a cluster, or collection, of galaxies known as the Local Group. These include Andromeda, the Triangulam galaxy, and Canis Major Dwarf as well as another 40 galaxies, some of which have only recently been discovered. The Local Group has a diameter of about 10 million light-years.

3-second sum-up

Our sun is just 1 among 200 billion stars in the Milky Way.

3-minute mission Star Count

Let's assume that there are 200 billion stars in the Milky Way—yes, that's 200,000,000,000! How many years would it take to count them all, assuming you can count a star every second? These tips should help you:

1 Use a calculator. Work out how many stars you could count in a day.

2 Multiply your day figure by 365.25 (to allow for the leap year every four years).

Answer on page 96

The Milky Way
is a spiral galaxy.

At the center is
a supermassive
black hole.

Our sun

Our solar system
orbits the center
of the Milky Way.

Galaxies

... in 30 seconds

The universe contains large numbers of galaxies. Each is a vast collection of gas, dust, stars, and planets. Most are impossible to see from Earth because they are such huge distances away.

One of the Milky Way's nearest neighbors is the M31 Andromeda galaxy. Andromeda may be 220,000 light-years across and contain as many as 800 billion stars.

Andromeda is moving toward the Milky Way at a rapid rate—more than 87 miles (140 km) a second. However, don't let this keep you awake. Even at that speed, it will take more than 3 billion years for the two galaxies to reach each other.

Astronomers place galaxies into broad groups based on their overall shape. The Milky Way and Andromeda are both spiral galaxies. Other galaxies are elliptical—oval-shaped—or round.

Lenticular galaxies are flat disks, often with a bulge in the center. Galaxies with no obvious shape are called irregular. They were probably pulled out of shape by gravity from other galaxies.

3-second sum-up

A galaxy is a vast collection of gas, dust, stars, and planets.

3-minute mission Galaxy Shapes

Go to NASA's images Web site—http://www.nasaimages.org —select universe, and view a stunning selection of photos of distant galaxies.

1 Try to find two spiral galaxies besides Andromeda, the Whirlpool, and the Milky Way.
2 Is the M87 galaxy irregular, elliptical, or lenticular?
3 Is the M104 Sombrero galaxy irregular, spiral, or elliptical?

Spiral galaxy

Elliptical galaxy

Lenticular galaxy

Irregular galaxy

Black Holes

... in 30 seconds

No one has ever seen a black hole. It is a point in space where gravity is so strong that it pulls everything into it—all matter, gas, light, everything. A very dense mass in a tiny area generates this incredibly powerful gravity.

As far as we know, no object can ever escape from a black hole.

There is an area of space around a black hole from which light cannot escape. The very edge of this area is called the event horizon. Any energy or matter inside the event horizon cannot escape being drawn into the black hole's clutches.

Scientists believe that there are several types of black holes. Supermassive black holes are found in the center of galaxies. Stellar black holes are formed after a supernova leaves behind a large, incredibly dense star core (center). This large core keeps on collapsing in on itself, as the pull of gravity increases, until a black hole is formed.

3-second sum-up

Black holes suck in everything around them— even light.

How to See a Black Hole

If no light ever escapes from a black hole, how can we possibly see them? Excellent question.

Astronomers seek out black holes by measuring their effects on other bodies outside of them. For example, some black holes have been discovered by observing gas and dust from a star near a stellar black hole being pulled into them.

Whole planets disappear.

The black hole has an enormous gravitational pull.

Matter, gas, and light are all pulled in.

Everything within the event horizon is sucked into the black hole.

Are There Aliens?

... in 30 seconds

Does extraterrestrial life exist? No one knows for sure. Astronomers have scoured the solar system and beyond without detecting any aliens. Yet the chemical elements that make up life on Earth are found throughout the universe.

Given that the universe is phenomenally huge, is it probable that a small planet in a single galaxy contains the universe's only life?

The sheer scale of the universe makes searching for aliens extremely hard. However, some organizations scour radio telescope signals for signs of intelligent life. People have also tried to announce our presence to aliens. For example, radio signals that show key facts about Earth and humans have been beamed into space.

Some alien hunters are excited by the recent discovery of exoplanets—planets found orbiting stars other than the sun. More than 700 have been found so far. Could any have the right conditions for life to form?

3-second sum-up

No aliens have been found ... yet.

3-minute mission Contact Aliens

Imagine you are designing an image to be beamed out into the universe to make contact with alien life forms. What information would you include? How would you show it?

Aliens will not understand English. Think about symbols, signs, and images that could show them humans, the Earth, and its place in the universe.

There are 42 radio dishes, all 20 feet (6 m) across.

The dishes receive radio signals from space.

20 feet (6 m)

The Allen Telescope array seeks out radio signals from space that might be from aliens.

The radio dishes pivot to point to different patches of sky.

Plotting the Universe

Before the telescope was invented, scientists knew little about the stars and planets. From the sixteenth century on, scientists used telescopes to examine these bodies in more detail. Advances in the twentieth century helped humans, probes, and scientific instruments to journey into space for the first time. Now, telescopes and probes can send back amazingly detailed information about planets and moons across the solar system.

Plotting the Universe
Glossary

amplifier Equipment that makes sounds or radio signals stronger and louder.

antenna (plural antennae) Equipment made of wire or long straight pieces of metal for receiving or sending radio signals.

aperture Opening.

astronomer A scientist who studies the sun, moon, stars, planets, and space in general.

atmosphere The mixture of gases that surround a planet.

black hole An area in space that nothing can escape from, because **gravity** is so strong.

booster rocket The first stage of a rocket or additional rockets fitted to the main rocket. The booster rocket or rockets fire at launch time and drop away when their fuel is used up.

combustion A chemical reaction in which substances combine with oxygen to produce heat and light.

comet A mass of ice and dust that moves around the sun.

exoplanet A planet in another planetary system.

galaxy A grouping of stars, dust, and gas clouds that may also contain planets.

gravity A force that pulls objects in space toward each other. Around Earth, it pulls them toward the planet, so things fall to the ground when you drop them.

km/h Kilometers per hour; a measure of speed.

micrometeoroid A miniature meteoroid, a tiny piece of rock in space.

MMU A rocket-powered device that astronauts can wear so they can float freely in space.

mph Miles per hour; a measure of speed.

nebula (plural nebulae) A huge cloud of dust and gas. Some nebulae form stars.

neutron star A type of extremely dense star.

optical telescope A telescope that gathers in light through its opening and makes objects in space appear much larger.

orbit A curved path followed by a planet or an object as it moves around a planet or star. To orbit is to go around a planet or star.

oxidizer A chemical that releases oxygen.

radio wave A type of electromagnetic wave with a long wavelength, used for communication on Earth and given off by a number of bodies in space.

reflecting telescope A form of **telescope** using smooth, curved mirrors to gather and focus light, to make images from space look bigger.

refracting telescope A kind of **telescope** with lenses to bend and focus light to make images from space look bigger.

satellite A device sent into space that moves around Earth, the moon, or another planet. It is used for communication, research, and other tasks.

solar panel Equipment on space stations and some space probes that converts the sun's light energy into electricity.

space probe A spacecraft without people on board that obtains information and sends it back to Earth.

supernova, type II (plural supernovae) A star that suddenly becomes much brighter and gives out a huge amount of energy because it is exploding and dying.

telescope An instrument that gathers in light or other signals from space so people can study distant objects.

universe The whole of space and everything in it, including Earth, the other planets, and stars.

weightlessness Having no weight. Occurs when there is no gravity.

Optical Telescopes
... in 30 seconds

Optical telescopes gather in light from space through the aperture (opening). The first telescopes invented were refracting telescopes. They gather in far more light than a human eye. The light passes through a convex lens (it is thinner around the edges than in the center). This bends the light so that it comes together and focuses at a point inside the telescope. A second lens in the telescope spreads the focused image out across your eye so the image is magnified.

Scientists found that bigger apertures and lenses could magnify objects more, but larger lenses were really heavy, hard to make, and developed areas of color around their edges. A new form of telescope was developed using smooth, curved mirrors to gather and focus light. These reflecting telescopes can be astonishingly huge.

The Keck 1 and 2 telescopes on Hawaii each have mirrors made up of 36 separate segments that together have a diameter of 33 feet (10 m). These telescopes have amazing powers and are able to see objects millions of light-years away. Scientists have used Keck telescopes to discover many exoplanets—planets orbiting distant stars.

3-second sum-up

Optical telescopes magnify distant objects in space.

3-minute mission Make a Telescope

To make a simple telescope, find two plastic magnifying glass lenses, one bigger than the other. Hold one lens in each hand and place them in line, the bigger lens in front of the smaller.

Aim them at an object—a street light at dusk or nighttime is ideal—and look through them. Adjust the distance between the two lenses until your target object is nice and sharp.

Light enters through the aperture (opening).

Light bounces off the secondary mirror.

The tertiary (third) mirror directs light to the eyepiece.

Light hits the primary mirror, which helps to focus it onto the secondary mirror.

Eyepiece

Radio Telescopes

... in 30 seconds

In the early 1930s, an American radio engineer, Karl Jansky, discovered radio signals coming from the Milky Way. Sounding like static or noise, they were given off by a radio source called Sagittarius A*, coming from what we now believe is a black hole. Other radio waves are given off by gases in space, rotating neutron stars called pulsars, and some supernova remnants.

By studying the radio waves coming from these sources, astronomers can learn about the objects' structure, movement, and what they are made from.

Radio astronomy is useful because it is not affected by daylight, clouds, or rain. Radio waves can also travel through dust and can be used to study the hot, dusty nebulae in space.

Many radio telescopes use a series of small dishes linked together in an array.

3-second sum-up

Radio telescopes collect radio waves given off by objects in space.

Giant Dishes

Some radio telescopes are single giant dishes. The Arecibo telescope in Puerto Rico has a dish that is a staggering 1,000 feet (305 m) in diameter.

By about 2016, it will be dwarfed by a new dish in China. Called FAST, it will be 1,640 feet (500 m) wide. Its dish area will be bigger than 25 football fields! FAST will be three times more sensitive than the Arecibo dish.

Space Telescopes
... in 30 seconds

If you use an optical telescope on Earth, you have to peer through the Earth's atmosphere, which can absorb some waves and scatter light. Telescopes in space can produce sharp images of really distant parts of the universe. They can work around the clock, not just at night as they can on Earth.

The Hubble Space Telescope (HST) was launched in 1990. It has taken more than 700,000 images of space and relayed them back to Earth. In 1994, it tracked a comet that crashed into Jupiter.

The Hubble has shown us things in the universe we had never seen before. It helped to discover supermassive black holes and took images of exoplanets for the very first time.

One of Hubble's most famous photos is called the Hubble Ultra Deep Field (HUDF). Made from data gathered in 2003–04, it shows more than 10,000 galaxies, some as far back as 13 billion light-years—less than a billion years after the universe was formed.

3-second sum-up

Space telescopes show clear images of the universe across space and time.

Snapshot in Time

Light can take many millions or billions of years to travel from distant stars and galaxies to Earth.

This means that the view we get of a distant object is a history lesson. It shows the object as it was millions or billions of years earlier.

Rocket Science

... in 30 seconds

Spacecrafts need an enormous amount of power to lift off, overcome Earth's gravity and launch into space. A rocket is the launch vehicle.

In space, there is no oxygen to help burn fuel. So rocket engines carry their own fuel and an oxygen-producing chemical called an oxidizer. The fuel and oxidizer are mixed together, then burned in large combustion chambers to produce huge amounts of gases. As these gases expand rapidly out of the exhausts of the engine downward, the launch vehicle moves in the opposite direction, upward.

Some launch vehicles use booster rockets. These fire at launch time and drop away as soon as their fuel is used, removing weight from the launch vehicle. Other launch vehicles have two or three stages, each with their own rocket engine or engines. As each stage uses up its fuel, it falls away.

3-second sum-up

Rocket engines power launch vehicles and send them up into space.

3-minute mission **Launch a Rocket**

1 Blow up a long balloon, fold over the open end, and keep it shut with a clothespin.

2 Run a long thread through a drinking straw. Tape the straw to the side of the balloon.

3 Tape the end of the thread near the clothespin to the floor. Ask a friend to hold the other end as high as possible. Push the balloon down. Release the clothespin.

4 Lift off!

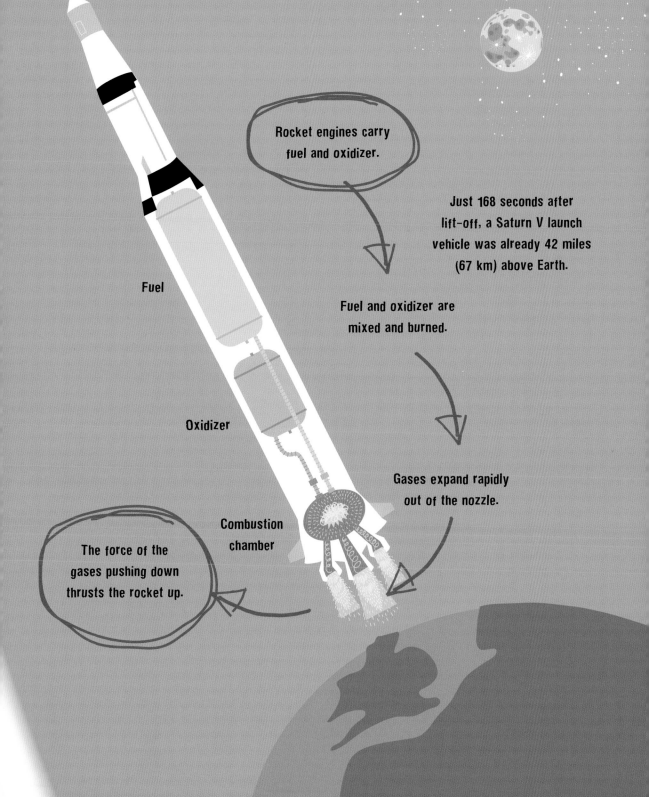

Space Probes

... in 30 seconds

Some probes have orbited or landed on planets or their moons. Others have flown by asteroids or comets. They send vital information gathered by their scientific instruments back to Earth via radio waves that travel at the speed of light.

Space probes mostly go on one-way missions, never returning to Earth. Without precious humans on board, some travel to hostile places and send back data until they're destroyed.

A handful of probes do return. Part of the Stardust probe came back in 2006 after its 1999 launch, with dust samples from the tail of the comet Wild 2.

The Mars Exploration Rover B (MER-B) was extraordinarily successful. After landing on Mars in January 2004, its mission was supposed to last 90 Martian days. The six-wheel, solar-powered rover managed to work for more than 30 times longer!

3-second sum-up

Space probes explore the solar system.

3-minute mission Space Probe Quiz

Go to the Cassini space probe Web page: http://saturn.jpl.nasa.gov/mission/quickfacts and answer these questions:

1 The Huygens probe landed on a Saturn moon that had the same name as the rocket that launched Cassini. Which was it?

2 How many Cassini probes equal the weight of its launch vehicle, a Titan rocket?

3 How many days from its launch did Cassini take to arrive at Saturn? Don't forget leap years!

Answer on page 96

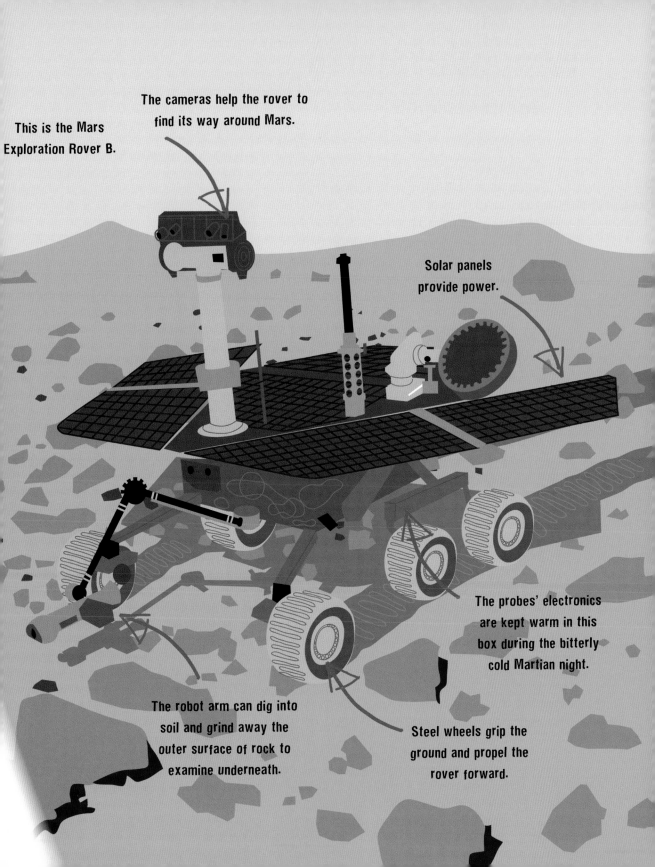

This is the Mars Exploration Rover B.

The cameras help the rover to find its way around Mars.

Solar panels provide power.

The probes' electronics are kept warm in this box during the bitterly cold Martian night.

The robot arm can dig into soil and grind away the outer surface of rock to examine underneath.

Steel wheels grip the ground and propel the rover forward.

Weightlessness

... in 30 seconds

Some astronauts spend long periods of time on spacecrafts such as the International Space Station.

Life in space poses special challenges for the human body. On Earth, gravity presses down on your skeleton, but when orbiting in space, astronauts experience weightlessness.

The weightlessness is because the spacecraft is falling through space. The disks between the bones of astronauts' spines expand a little, and they grow slightly taller.

Inside a spacecraft, you can't eat normally. Food crumbs would float away, fouling up instruments and making a terrible mess. Astronauts eat specially designed food. They have high-tech toilets, with air to flush away waste. Astronauts shower in a sealed shower pod and afterward, air sucks away the water droplets.

3-second sum-up

In space, humans experience weightlessness.

3-minute mission **Match the Milestones**

Match the astronauts (right) to their space milestones (left).

First person in space, 1961	**John Glenn**
First woman in space, 1963	**Susan J. Helms and James S. Voss**
Most time in space	
First spacewalk, 1965	**Sergei Krikalev**
Longest single spacewalk: 8 hours, 56 minutes, 2001	**Valentina Tereshkova**
	Yuri Gargarin
Oldest astronaut: 77 years, 1998	**Alexei Leonov**

Answer on page 96

Space Suits

... in 30 seconds

Space is a hostile place for humans. Tiny particles called micrometeoroids can whiz by at speeds fast enough to rip through flesh. There's no air to breathe. You get extremely hot in the sunlight and freezing cold in shadow.

Modern spacecrafts contain air, so astronauts can wear normal clothes. For lift-off from Earth and trips outside the spacecraft, they wear space suits.

First, the astronaut puts on a maximum absorption garment (an adult diaper) because there are no toilets in outer space. He or she also puts on special water-cooled underwear. Next is an electrical harness that contains all the circuits and wiring for the radio and devices that monitor the astronaut's health.

The main suit is white to reflect the sun's heat energy. It is thick to stop injury from particles whizzing by. The suit is linked to a backpack, the Primary Life Support System (PLSS). This controls the temperature inside the suit and provides oxygen and electricity for the suit's electrical parts.

3-second sum-up

A space suit is a complete life-support system for an astronaut.

Spacewalks

Astronauts go on extravehicular activities (EVAs), or spacewalks, to do space experiments, capture a satellite, or to check or repair a spacecraft.

The astronaut is usually connected to the outside of the spacecraft by a tether. However, the MMU, a rocket-powered device used in 1984, allowed for astronauts to fly freely in space.

The helmet contains lights, digital cameras, and a radio for talking to the rest of the crew.

The astronaut wears special gloves with small heaters over each fingertip.

Astronauts in space wear high-tech diapers.

The space suit has a plastic pouch with water to sip via a tube in the helmet.

The boots have soft soles to avoid damaging fragile spacecraft parts.

International Space Station
... in 30 seconds

The International Space Station (ISS) is the largest space station to be launched. It is four times bigger than the Russian Mir space station launched in 1986. Since 1998, 100 missions from Earth have built it up, module by module.

Giant solar array wings (SAWs) provide electrical power for the ISS. Each wing has an area greater than 2,200 square feet (300 square meters) and 32,800 solar cells to convert the sun's energy into electricity.

Inside the ISS are crew quarters, places for visiting spacecraft to dock, two bathrooms, an exercise gym, and plenty of working areas as well as storage places for tools, supplies, and experiments.

Hundreds of different science experiments are performed on the ISS. Some are about the effects of weightlessness on materials and creatures, while others are to examine Earth below or to learn more about humans in space.

3-second sum-up

A space station the size of a football field orbits 250 miles (400 km) above Earth.

ISS—the Stats

Built by: the United States, Russia, Japan, Canada, and the European Space Agency

Length: 240 feet (74 m)

Width: 36 feet (110 m)

Orbital speed: Around 17,200 mph (27,700 km/h)

Expeditions: 31 (by 2012)

Distance traveled: More than 1.7 million miles (2.8 million km)

First crew: Expedition 1 (2000) spent 136 days on board

Operational life: up to 2020 or 2028

Solar array wings provide electricity.

The living module is home for the astronauts.

Astronauts carry out research in the experiment module.

Nodes (corridor links) connect the experiment and living modules.

Discover More

NONFICTION BOOKS

13 Planets: The Latest View of the solar system by David A. Aguilar
National Geographic Society, 2011

Black Holes by Ker Than
Children's Press, 2010

Book of Astronomy and Space by Lisa Miles and Alastair Smith
Usborne, 2009

The Comic Strip History of Space by Tracey Turner
Bloomsbury, 2009

First Encyclopedia of Space by Paul Dowsell
Usborne, 2010

The Everything Kids Astronomy Book by Kathi Wagner
Adams, 2008

Out of this World: All the Cool Bits about Space by Clive Gifford
Buster Books, 2011

The Pop Up, Pull Out Space Book
Dorling Kindersley, 2010

Science: Sorted! Space, Black Holes and Stuff by Glenn Murphy
Macmillan Children's Books, 2010

*See Inside Space (See Inside):
With over 50 flaps to lift & a little book of Star Maps* by Katie Daynes
Usborne, 2008

Space: A Children's Encyclopedia
Dorling Kindersley, 2010

Spacecraft and the Journey into Space by Raman Prinja
QED Publishing, 2012

DVDs—suitable for all ages

Discovery Channel—NASA's Greatest Missions Go Entertain, 2009

Earth and Space History Channel, 2011

Wonders of the solar system, starring Brian Cox
2entertain, 2010

WEB SITES

Amazing Space
http://amazing-space.stsci.edu
All about the universe, using Hubble Space Telescope's discoveries

Esa Kids
www.esa.int/esaKIDSen/
European Space Agency site about our universe and life in space

Eyes on the solar system
http://eyes.nasa.gov/index.html
A site full of real NASA mission data

Kids Astronomy
www.kidsastronomy.com
Information about space and exploration, and games

Mars Exploration Program
http://marsprogram.jpl.nasa.gov/participate/funzone/
All about Mars and missions to Mars, with games

The Space Place
http://spaceplace.nasa.gov
Facts, activities, and games from NASA

Index